Dog Heraldry

The Official Collection of Canine Coats of Arms

NON DISPUTARE ILLEGITIMUS

by
Mia Martin

HOWELL
BOOK
HOUSE

New York

Howell Book House
Macmillan General Reference
A Simon & Schuster Macmillan Company
1633 Broadway
New York, NY 10019

Library of Congress Cataloging-in-Publication Data
Martin, Mia
    Dog heraldry: the official collection of canine coats-of-arms/
  by Mia Martin
       p.   cm.
     ISBN 0-87605-532-3
     1. Dog breeds.   2. Heraldry, Ornamental.   I. Title
   SF426.M38   1996
   929.8'2--dc20   95-52289
                                                           CIP

Manufactured in the United States of America
10 9 8 7 6 5 4 3 2 1

Dedication

To my mother and father, the most wonderful and loving parents a child could have. And to the rest of my family for putting up with all my woofs!

About the Author

Mia Pierpont Martin has studied the art and origins of heraldry for the past decade. She developed a keen interest in history and the arts as a student at Franklin College in Switzerland and the Corcoran School of Art in Washington, D.C. A native of the Virginia hunt country, she has always had a deep interest in animals. She currently resides with her pets in New York.

Contents

Contents

Acknowledgments

First and most important, Bob Walton, a dear friend whose great vision helped make this book possible. Thank you!

I would also like to thank Cliff de Raita, a friend whose dog world knowledge has been invaluable.

Charles Hunt who started me off on the right path.

Sean Frawley, president and publisher of Howell Book House, for giving me this opportunity and my editors, Felice Primeau and Ariel Cannon, whose enthusiasm for the book opened the door for me. Without their patience I could not have succeeded.

Susan Gray, a great friend and talented photographer whose opinions, support and direction have meant a great deal to me.

Mr. and Mrs. Frederick W. Wagner, III, and "Chester."

Charles Finch whose ideas were greatly appreciated.

Danielle Kazmier for her sound advice.

Marilou Stannard Doyle and Mrs. Charles Bartlett for their guidance and support.

Fluffy, for her spiritual uplift.

Lian McCallister, Murray Altchular and Steve Elkman, all of whom helped point me in the right direction.

I offer a special thanks to Belinda Brackenridge and "the Bear."

Foreword

If I had been born of nobility I would be deeply offended by Mia Martin's *Dog Heraldry,* but since I was not born of nobility and was apparently stolen by vagabonds from a rather middle-class farming community somewhere in Eastern Europe, I am not offended by Mia Martin. In fact, I am absolutely delighted with her. I think this book is fun, in fact it is a positive romp, and I think it's overdue. It's about time that we recognize the true nobility of our canine companions. They have, after all, been ruining our shrubs and chewing our needlework cushions for a hundred and forty centuries. And now at last we're acknowledging them in an appropriate way. Who says that human beings are slow! It only took us from the Stone Age until now to lock step with history.

I don't think I've ever met a dog that didn't deserve its own coat of arms, although I've met very few people who do. Mia Martin has put all of this in perspective. Our most worthy friends get their due and the world gets a wonderful new art form and concept.

Mia Martin has an eye for the essence of dog, dogdom, and dogginess without being dogged or resorting to doggerel. I think that is about as much as you can say for someone, because in so doing, you are acknowledging that that person is wise. And when a person is both wise and funny and loves dogs, you have an unbeatable combination, and such is *Dog Heraldry.* Frankly, I feel very good about the whole thing, doggone it.

Roger A. Caras
Thistle Hill Farm
President
ASPCA

❧ Introduction ❧

Heraldry is the ancient art of designing unique symbols that identify specific individuals or organizations. Over the centuries, elaborate customs, traditions and rules have developed in regard to how these symbols are placed, colored and designed, and as to what specific devices mean in coats of arms. Unless you are seriously interested in all of that, the simple diagram presented here is all you really need to know, so I won't go into deep detail. Suffice it to say that this collection of coats of arms reflects the highest standards of heraldry.

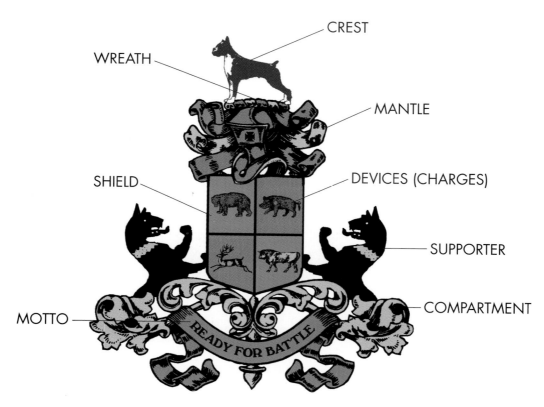

CREST

WREATH

MANTLE

SHIELD

DEVICES (CHARGES)

SUPPORTER

COMPARTMENT

MOTTO

READY FOR BATTLE

Symbols of one kind or another have been used for identification ever since people first began to draw. For example, a "chop," a unique symbol carved on the end of a stick to be used like a rubber stamp, has been employed since the dawn of time by the Chinese to identify themselves. (Fingerprints might be considered nature's form of "chop.") These symbols became increasingly elaborate for those who obtained high recognition and frequently extended to cover all the members of a family, tribe, country or other organization. Around the 11th century, when the use of complete body armor became fashionable, it was difficult to distinguish friend from foe; faces were invisible with the helmet visor down. So knights began painting designs on their shields to let others know who they were. This led to intense competition among the sign painters who, like artists throughout time, worked hard to create the best design for their customers. Copyright laws were not too prevalent back then, so these sign painters, or heralds, got together to register their work and prevent others from using it. They established whatever rules they wanted "to maintain standards." One rule was that not everyone was allowed to have a sign on their shield. This made them exclusive and, therefore, in great demand.

Another problem quickly became apparent to those who dressed up in their shiny new suits of armor and rode out into battle. The things had neither heat nor air conditioning. The knights would freeze in winter and roast in summer. To shade themselves from the sun or keep out the cold, the knights draped their armor with cloth. They had coats made for their armor and these coats were identified by the custom tailors of the day as "coats of arms." Tailors are just as competitive as sign painters and they recognized a good thing when they saw it. They took the heralds' designs and embroidered them on the coats of arms. These exclusive and increasingly elaborate designs became important status symbols, so the royalty and nobility who were entitled to them wanted to show them off. Not only were they displayed on armor and shield, they were copied onto every conceivable object from signet rings to castles. And they still are.

Pictures of dogs have long been used in coats of arms and other logos but, like the common man, dogs were not entitled to their own coats of arms. Until now. The purpose of this book is to rectify that injustice. So it is with great pleasure that this collection is presented to the dogs of the world. They can now join the ranks of the elite and carry their noses as high as their coats of arms. My apologies to those dogs who are not represented here, but their time will come, I promise.

DIABLOTIN MOUSTACHU

${\mathcal A}$ffenpinscher

There may be no older toy dog than the Affenpinscher. Primarily a ratter, he is also an expert rabbit hunter. His name comes from the German word for monkey, *Affe*, as his face is said to be monkeyish. At times he is also referred to as the "mustached little devil" (*Diablotin Moustachu*) because of the way the hair grows on his face. Be that as it may, the Affenpinscher is a sterling example of a Teutonic dog. The breed's coat of arms contains both the German cross on an ancient Teutonic helmet and the German Eagle. Two monkeys serve as supporters for the shield which contains rabbits and rats.

ﬄfghan Hound

The Afghan Hound is the most aloof, dignified and aristocratic of canine breeds. In addition to her regal bearing, she is also a fine hunter, relying on superb sight to spot and track prey. The western world first noticed this dog in Afghanistan, where kings had been keeping kennels of them for centuries. The Afghan Hound could easily outdistance horse and rider to bring to bay quarry from rabbit to gazelle. Therefore, her coat of arms bears a gazelle, rabbit and desert hunter on horseback. Game and a hunter are figured as supporters.

FLEET, FIERCE, FAITHFUL

$\mathfrak{A}$iredale Terrier

The Airedale Terrier is a formidable and versatile hunter. He has hunted creatures from the smallest water rat to the greatest game, everywhere from the game lands of America and Canada to India and Africa. But what really attracts his owners is his endearing personality, faithful companionship and watchful protectiveness. His shield has room for only a small sample of his prey: elk, bear, badger, boar and fox.

Akita

The Akita is one of the Magnificent Seven: seven dog breeds designated as national monuments in Japan. The Akita is known as "*Matagi-Inu*," or esteemed hunting dog. Bear, boar and deer were her primary targets and at one time ownership was restricted to the aristocracy for use on their private hunting preserves. Samurai warriors, also a favorite of the aristocracy, support her shield.

POWERFUL AND LOYAL

Alaskan Malamute

Among sled dogs, the Alaskan Malamute is one of the oldest breeds and arguably the strongest, though not necessarily the swiftest. The Inuit tribe known as Mahlemuts employed this sturdy breed as loyal protectors of their caribou herds. He also earned his keep by hunting polar bears, a food he enjoyed as much as his masters. More recently, his earning power expanded into commercial territory as a Rent-a-Sled-Dog for European Arctic explorers.

FRIEND AND GUARDIAN

ᴀmerican Eskimo Dog

Now here is a real American dog, born and bred in the U.S.A. The breed was given the title of Eskimo in honor of the native Alaskans, who helped establish this dog as a favorite pet. She is not usually a sled dog, but she could be—she has the heart and enthusiasm for the task. Like other Northern dogs, the American Eskimo dog has a cheerful expression and a face that could launch a thousand ships. No matter what is expected of her, she excels as a congenial family member and faithful companion.

EXITUS ACTA PROBAT

George Washington

American Foxhound

George Washington's coat of arms fittingly appears on the shield of the American Foxhound. Washington played a significant role in the development of both the breed and of fox hunting in America. In pre-Revolutionary War days he imported dogs from France and England to his Virginia kennels and remained an ardent fox hunter and hound breeder all his life. Wily foxes support the shield of this early American canine.

American Staffordshire Terrier

The American Staffordshire Terrier is an all American dog. A cross between the Bulldog and terrier breeds, she was at first unoriginally called the Bull-and-Terrier Dog. In the era of dog fights, this breed was continually a winner. She is now known for her loyal protection of hearth and home as well as her gentleness with children.

American Water Spaniel

The American Water Spaniel is an all around hunting dog developed in the United States. His coat of arms reflects both his origins and talents. A U.S. shield is surrounded by other devices that depict the variety of game which the American Water Spaniel helps to hunt. His specially bred talent of retrieving from small boats is depicted in another device. The shield is supported by two ancient heraldic spaniels.

GOOD, STRONG, SELF-SUFFICIENT AUSSIE

Australian Cattle Dog

The Australian Cattle Dog (Aucado) was over sixty years in the making. The imported European herding dogs were unable to deal with the Australian cattle spread over vast territories. The native dingo dog was capable, but could not be domesticated. After years of crossbreeding dingoes with several varieties of European dogs, the Aucado was finally perfected in the 1890s. The breed's shield is a simple one: Australian symbols on a barren landscape base with, naturally, kangaroos for supporters. The Australian Cattle Dog is a good, hearty and self-sufficient Aussie.

GOOD AS TWO MEN ON HORSEBACK

Australian Kelpie

Some say that Australia may never have amounted to much if it were not for the Kelpie, its sheep dog *par excellence*. She is a pure Scottish immigrant and is as canny a workaholic as any Scot. (Mind you she is a teetotaler.) Hence the symbol of Scotland appears on her shield. The shield shows two sheep, though she is a superior cattle driver as well.

PLAYFUL AND COURAGEOUS

Australian Terrier

Accompanying the English prisoners transported to Australia in the late 1800s was a dog known as the Rough-Coated Terrier. It was well suited for the rough company it was in. It thrived in Tasmania where the most incorrigible prisoners were sent. There the terriers crossbred with other dogs, eventually developing into the rough and tumble, fearless little dog that the Australian Terrier is today. Not your placid house pet, this intrepid terrier kills snakes and rats, serves as a burglar alarm and works equally well on waterfronts and sheep and cattle farms.

He likes people (his family in particular) and takes good care of them. His coat of arms reflects these occupations, and is supported by symbolic kangaroos of Australia.

12

Basenji

A native of Central Africa, the Basenji, or "barkless dog," is among the oldest known dog breeds. To this day the Basenji is a smart, fast and silent pointer, retriever and game driver. They were given as gifts to the Pharaohs of Ancient Egypt and are depicted in paintings of that era. This history is reflected in the coat of arms which shows the pyramids, King Tut and an ancient drawing of the dog. The shield is supported by Central African elephants. The motto speaks for itself (the Basenji cannot speak for herself—she is barkless after all).

SLOWLY BUT SURELY

ℬasset Hound

Although the Basset Hound may have originated in Constantinople, the breed is more aptly described as a product of France. As a hunting dog of the aristocracy, he was valued chiefly for his excellence in chasing both rabbit and hare for shooting. The English took a fancy to the Basset; later Americans taught him to tree possum and coon. Although some consider the Basset to be the laziest of dogs, he really only strives to conserve his energy for the chase and should not be misjudged on the basis of his rather lugubrious appearance.

TIRELESS AND DETERMINED

ℬeagle

The Beagle looks like a small Foxhound, but came into her own much earlier. In fact, the beagle was bred with others to produce the Foxhound when fox hunting became popular in the 18th century. The Beagle prefers to hunt rabbit or hare, tirelessly chasing them by herself or in a pack. Like most great hunters, at home she is gentle and trustworthy.

Bearded Collie

Descended from the Magyar Komondor, the Bearded Collie is not of noble ancestry. He was always a humble working dog who was, and still is, excellent at driving both cattle and sheep. Bearded Collies were so highly prized in Scotland that puppies were given only to homes that would work them. He is given the place of honor in the center of a royal Scottish shield supported by a Highland shepherd and a hefty ram.

Bedlington Terrier

The Bedlington Terrier's svelte appearance tends to hide her great courage, energy and speed. These traits made the breed appealing to poachers (among others), and this terrier was originally kept by gypsies for this purpose. Like most terriers, she is a good ratter and exterminator of other vermin including badger, fox and otter. This gentle dog was on occasion matched against other dogs in fights to the death, but now enjoys a more appropriate role as a loving family pet.

Belgian Malinois

Belgium has chosen not to establish a single language, so everything is labeled bilingually. In keeping with this diverse tradition, they selected not two, but three breeds of sheepdog to be the standards of their *Chien de Berger Belge:* the Belgian Tervuren, the Belgian Sheepdog and the Belgian Malinois.

Here is the Belgian Malinois, distinguished from the others by its short, fawn colored hair and its black mask. The coat of arms contains a shield surmounted by the lion of Belgium surrounded by a selection of sheep. A farm fence is used as a crest with the dog above. This is all supported by a pair of ancient heraldic rams. This crest is shared with the other two *Chiens de Berger Belge.*

ℬelgian Sheepdog

And now the Belgian Sheepdog. This is the black, long-haired version. His coat of arms is shared with the other two *Chiens de Berger Belge*.

Belgian Tervuren

The Belgian Tervuren is called after the village of that name. This is a long-haired dog that is not black. The coat of arms is shared with the other two *Chiens de Berger Belge.*

ℬernese Mountain Dog

This big, strong dog is affectionately called "The Bear Cub." An ancient Roman war dog, he accompanied invading Roman soldiers into Switzerland where he was quickly adopted by Swiss farmers and put to work. (Swords into ploughshares, so to speak.) He guarded and herded animal stock in addition to serving as a draft animal. His image crests the shield of Bern, Switzerland.

ALWAYS CHEERFUL

Bichon Frise

Many countries would be glad to claim the Bichon Frise as their own because of its incredible charm and cheerfulness. In fact, the breed originated in the Mediterranean region and was carried to the Canary Island, Teneriffe, centuries ago. It was brought to Europe in the 14th century and established as Franco-Belgian. The great charm of this little dog has ensured it a life of leisure, supported by devoted owners.

ℬlack and Tan Coonhound

The Black and Tan, or just plain ol' Coonhound has been shuffling around in one form or another since the English Talbot Hound of the 11th century. Bloodhounds and Foxhounds, both English and American, crept into the line, finally resulting in this incomparable hound dog. Hunting entirely by scent, he is a dog that truly keeps his nose to the grindstone.

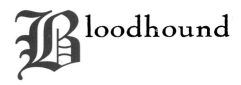

$\mathfrak{B}$loodhound

The Bloodhound! This intrepid detective will follow the scent of a suspect for hundreds of miles to bring him to justice. Who would suspect that it is one of the most gentle and affectionate of dogs? Although it tracks its quarry relentlessly, it never attacks or harms in any way.

One explanation for its name is that it was much prized by European aristocrats (blue bloods) and was hence known as the "blooded" hound. Its shield reflects its ancient origin in Constantinople and establishment in Belgium (represented by the Belgian Lion and the Royal Crown).

Border Collie

This Scottish dog exudes energy from its backwardly braced stance to its hypnotic stare—the famous "eye" that can will sheep to move. Border Collies are happiest tending to their chores. They love work and if none is given to them, they will search it out—true self-starting workaholics. If they have no animals to herd, they will round up the children and even, it is said, coconuts where available! They are always on the go. Needless to say, their owners need to be energetic, too.

ℬorder Terrier

Originating in the Cheviot Hills between Scotland and England, this "working terrier" is called the Border Terrier. This somewhat scruffy looking terrier can keep up with horses and a fox hunting pack, and lets no obstacle prevent him from following the fox to ground. It will also go after otter, badger, marten and other vermin. This dog is truly "hard as nails and game as they come."

ℬorzoi

Extremely fast and courageous, yet quiet and gentle, the Borzoi was bred by the Russian aristocracy even before the first Czar came to power. Not only is she an elegant and graceful pet, but her superb vision and speed make her unsurpassed for coursing wild game in the open. A common target was once the wolf, which the Borzoi pursued in ceremonial hunts staged by aristocrats as a display of wealth. The breed's historic name was the Russian Wolfhound. Here the Borzoi graces the shield of Imperial Russia.

$\mathfrak{B}$oston Terrier

In the 1920s, the Boston Terrier was considered the King of American Purebreds. His stance and chest markings are reminiscent of an elegant gentleman in formal dress. Though originally bred in America for dogfighting, the Boston Terrier is of gentle disposition and highly intelligent. Its shield carries pictures of two primary ancestors, the Bulldog and Bull Terrier, along with the American symbol, the eagle.

TOUCHEUR DE BOEUF

Bouvier des Flandres

The seemingly elegant name *Bouvier des Flandres* is actually an accurate description of this dog. *Bouvier* means ox driver or cow herder—both of which are talents of the breed. The dog originally came from provinces of Flandres, which once covered some of the Netherlands and France—hence the name Bouvier des Flandres. Once called "dirty beard" and "cow dog," the Bouvier is big and strong enough to pull farm carts with ease and makes an excellent watchdog.

ℬoxer

A courageous and devoted guard dog, the Boxer is of ancient Tibetan lineage and was developed to perfection in the 20th century in Germany. The pugilistic name comes from her peculiar fighting stance in which she raises her front paws. For a time, the Boxer participated in boar hunts and stag hunts, and was a fearless dog fighter and bull baiter. These activities are reflected in the shield, supported by ancient heraldic devices portraying the dog's fighting posture.

A HEART WRAPPED IN FUR

$\mathcal{B}$riard

The French Briard is so fearless, tough and intelligent that the breed was designated the official dog of the French army. During peacetime he has defended flocks and herds from wolves and poachers. In addition to his guarding instincts, he is also affectionate, loyal and obedient. He is often described as "a heart wrapped in fur."

Brittany

Originally registered as the "Spaniel Brittany," this bird dog with a superb nose could not choose between retrieving and pointing, so it does both magnificently. The name was shortened to the simpler "Brittany." No one knows for sure whether this refers to Great Britain or the French province of Brittany. The dog doesn't care and lives to this day in both places. Esteemed for woodcock hunting, he does just as well with other game birds like quail and partridge. His shield bears the shield of the Duke of Brittany as a heraldic device; the herald leans to France as the originator of the breed.

TOUJOURS FIDELE

Brussels Griffon

A self-important little rat catcher, the Brussels Griffon is a smart, alert and sensitive companion who, in another era, loved to perch proudly beside the driver of an elegant coach. The dog perches equally proudly upon the coat of arms of the city of Brussels, Belgium.

Bull Terrier

The Bull Terrier is a distinctive breed that comes in two varieties: white and colored. All Bull Terriers are very muscular, with an unforgettably powerful head. Long ago, when dog fighting was both a legal and popular sport, this breed was the gentleman's canine gladiator. The white variety is known even now as the "White Cavalier." Although descended from the Bulldog, another fighter, its appearance is quite different.

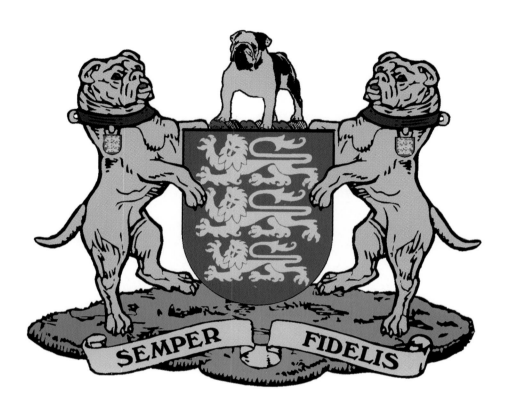

ℬulldog

Ah, the mighty Bulldog! Symbol of tenacity throughout the world. An ancient Briton who can snore with the best of them, the Bulldog was a vigorous and courageous fighter not only of other dogs, but also bulls and bears. In addition to being a symbol of Great Britain, the Bulldog proudly serves as the official United States Marine Corps mascot as well as the mascot of Yale University. Despite great popularity in the U.S., the dog's image accurately stands on an old English shield. The proud motto, that of the Marine Corps, describes its character.

GAMEKEEPERS NIGHTDOG

$\mathcal{B}$ullmastiff

The Bullmastiff is an awesome dog who was best avoided by the poachers for whom he was continuously on watch. He was the "Gamekeepers Night Dog" and would fearlessly attack on command after silently observing poachers creeping by. Captives were not bitten or mauled. Instead, the Bullmastiff would knock them to the ground, repeatedly if necessary, until the gamekeeper arrived. This dog was bred from a cross of Mastiff and Bulldog specifically for the purpose of guarding large English estates, so it proudly and appropriately wears a British coat of arms.

BOLD AND READY

Cairn Terrier

Is this a terrier or is this a terrier? The Cairn Terrier is the
very picture of a gnarled, bearded Scot who has worked for a
living from his earliest days on the Isle of Skye. The name
comes from cairns, the man-made piles of rocks marking land
boundaries that over the years became infested with vermin.
This terrier was employed by Scottish chieftains to roust out
and exterminate the vermin, which he fearlessly and
energetically did.

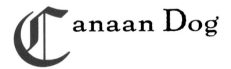

Canaan Dog

The Canaan Dog of Israel makes its living guarding and herding cattle and sheep. In times of war it fulfills its duty in the Israeli Army as a messenger and locator of wounded soldiers. It originated in the "Land of Canaan," and is depicted in drawings from about 2000 B.C. in the tombs at Beni–Hassan. Those drawings are depicted in its shield which also contains the symbol of Israel.

Cavalier King Charles Spaniel

The Cavalier King Charles Spaniel was rescued from oblivion by a club started by Roswell Eldridge in 1928. Over the following fifteen years, this classic breed was reestablished from genetic stock that still remained in the English Marlborough spaniels of Blenheim. It was no easy task, but one well done. This truly elegant and regal dog has now recovered its rightful place.

Chesapeake Bay Retriever

At the beginning of the 19th century, ancestors of the Chesapeake Bay Retriever arrived on the coast of Maryland from England by way of Newfoundland. The Chesapeake Bay is noted for ducks and geese which were numerous enough to sustain commercial hunting. This big, strong dog with her waterproof coat was ideally suited to the frigid waters of the bay where she could retrieve as many as 200 ducks a day—a true working dog. Her shield contains the Maryland state flag and devices reflecting her hunting activities, supported by foliage representative of the bay shores.

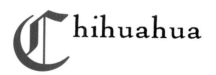

Chihuahua

Ancestors of the Chihuahua, known as "Techichi," existed in Mexico at least as far back as the 9th century and took part in the religious ceremonies of the Toltec and Aztec civilizations. Discovered by the Spanish conquistadors in the Mexican state of Chihuahua, this dog comes in two flavors: smooth coat and long coat. The smooth type is shown as the crest on the official coat of arms of the state of Chihuahua.

Hairless

Powderpuff

Chinese Crested

It's hard to believe, but the little Chinese Crested was once a working dog! For centuries these dogs roamed the world on Chinese ships, catching the rats that hid on board and carrying the fleas that spread the plague. The two varieties, "Hairless" and "Powderpuff" look quite different but share *most* characteristics, as well as the same coat of arms.

LORDLY   SNOBBISH   CONFIDENT

Chinese Shar-Pei

The Shar-Pei is an old Chinese working dog that hunted and herded for peasants. Despite his humble beginnings, he appears not only dignified and confident, but also "regal, lordly, and snobbish." His extremely loose skin brought him renown as a fighting dog. An opponent trying to bite would only get a mouthful of skin, while the Shar-Pei could still wriggle and fight within his loose coat.

Chow Chow

It may be hard to believe that this fuzzy, cuddly dog has a strong-man reputation. Sometimes called "Wolf Dog," and "Bear Dog," the Chow Chow was used in China for centuries as a bird dog for pheasant and general hunting dog. A T'ang emperor in the 7th century had a kennel housing 5,000 Chows. They were fierce guardians of family, herds, homes and property, as well as harness dogs for sleds and carts. Their name, however, is not Chinese, but pidgin–English. It was used by boat captains when describing all Chinese cargo, including their canine passengers. The coat of arms reflects the Chow Chow's Chinese history.

44

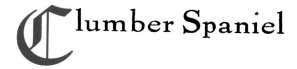

SLOW BUT SURE

Clumber Spaniel

Talk about name dropping! The Clumber Spaniel can do it in spades—the king of spades even. British royal and noble admirers included Prince Albert (consort to Queen Victoria), King Edward VII, King George V, the Duke of Newcastle at Clumber Park, the Duke of Portland, Lord Arthur Cecil and Earl Spencer. The Clumber Spaniel is a quiet hunter who can approach game very closely. He will hunt his fields tirelessly although, some say, rather slowly. He deserves to be the centerpiece of a royal coat of arms.

Cocker Spaniel

The Cocker Spaniel is an American product, and like so many Americans, more a weekend athlete than a regular one. She tends to spend most of her time lounging around home as a treasured pet and goes hunting with her owner only occasionally, even though she is often a far better hunter than her master. Her English Spaniel cousins are much bigger and perhaps more regular hunting dogs. The woodcock was a favorite prey (hence the name Cocker Spaniel) and it appears as a heraldic device on the shield. It is accompanied by a hunter and two generic heraldic spaniel supports.

ELEGANT LOYAL AFFECTIONATE

ℭollie

Though now known as an elegantly coifed movie star, the Collie
has historically been a hard working cattle and sheep driver.
Queen Victoria raised this dog from his humble shepherding
life in Scotland to that of "playmate to the rich and royal." His
shield bears the Scottish emblem, supported by a shepherd
and his dog and surmounted by a farm gate and another rough
Collie.

Curly Coated Retriever

The Curly Coated Retriever is at least as happy in the water as it is on land. Although it originated in England, this large, lovable dog has found its true home in New Zealand and Australia as a favorite retriever of duck and quail. Its shield bears the flags of those countries along with the birds it helps to hunt.

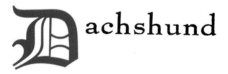

HARDY AND TIRELESS

Dachshund

It is a bum rap that Dachshunds are just spoiled and pampered pets. Spoiled and pampered they may be but with good reason—they are so lovable and affectionate. One should never forget, however, that they are Teutonic. Their name is German: *Dachs* (badger), and *hund* (dog). They tracked down badgers and rabbits using their specialized long, low bodies to pursue their quarry into tunnels.

The coat of arms is a shield with the three varieties: long-haired, wire-haired and smooth. It is crested by an ancient Teutonic helmet surmounted by a heraldic badger and supported by a pair of boars, which this breed also hunted fearlessly.

THE CARRIAGE DOG

Dalmatian

The Dalmatian is an excellent hunting dog, but its unique affinity to horses and distinguished appearance made it a favorite for accompanying carriages to protect travelers from highwaymen. She was also adopted by fire departments and rode to fires on the horse drawn wagons. Though horses have been replaced with engines, many fire stations still keep Dalmatians as mascots. She perches on the coat of arms of a coach makers' guild, which has been modified to bear the symbol of her place of origin—the Dalmatian Coast, Yugoslavia.

Dandie Dinmont Terrier

This is likely the only dog breed named after a fictional character, Dandie Dinmont, a farmer created by Sir Walter Scott in his book, *Guy Mannering*. This character kept a six member family of these dogs of which Sir Walter wrote, "...they fear naething that ever cam' wi' a hairy skin on't." They are true terriers from the border country between England and Scotland, where they were particularly expert in hunting otter and badger. They also confidently dispatched rabbit, rats and vermin of all sorts. All this and kind to children, too! The Dandie Dinmont Terrier stands proudly atop the crest of a British coat of arms which bears an otter and a badger.

Doberman Pinscher

Considering the attitude people have toward tax collectors, it seems reasonable that tax men might require personal bodyguards. Tax collector Louis Doberman of Apolda, Germany, decided he needed a fierce ally, and what could be better qualified than his "Doberman" Pinscher? Not many tax evaders would dare tangle with a dog that merely needs to look at someone to pacify him. The coat of arms reflects the authority of the Teutonic government for which the dogs worked, and shows his noble carriage and alertness. Note that when not working the Doberman Pinscher is a true family dog that loves his home.

COURAGE & DEVOTION

Cnglish Cocker Spaniel

Descended from hunting dogs of Spain (*Span*iels), the English Cocker Spaniel is arguably the finest of the small hunting dogs, and he excels in flushing woodcock (hence his name). The English Cocker Spaniel is considerably larger than the American breed. On the coat of arms, his picture surmounts the crest of a shield that bears the ancient English symbol of three lions, surrounded by shooters and woodcock.

KEEP WITH THE PACK

English Foxhound

England is justly proud of its talent in organizing, training and perfecting highly specialized groups to perform desirable functions—for example, the Beefeaters who guard the Tower of London. When hunting foxes became a favorite sport in the 18th century, *all* participants were properly trained and outfitted, not only the riders. The dogs were grouped into organized packs to locate and chase foxes. The result of this effort in breeding, training and perfection is the English Foxhound. The shield bears the heraldic lions of England and devices reflecting the "riding to hounds" in foxhunting.

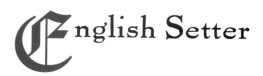

Cnglish Setter

The English Setter, of a sweet and mild disposition, is an outstanding English bird dog that "sets" game by positioning its body with its head towards the bird, preparing it for the sportsman's gun. Its elegant, aristocratic looks make it a fitting companion to the lion and unicorn of Great Britain.

English Springer Spaniel

This descendant of Spanish hunting dogs is closely related to the English Cocker Spaniel, though is somewhat larger. It has always had a single purpose—to hunt. It has a characteristic hunting style of springing to flush game out of cover. The stately English Springer Spaniel crests the shield of its coat of arms, which bears the heraldic lions of England surrounded by favorite game birds: pheasant, grouse, partridge and woodcock. It is supported by old heraldic spaniel dogs representing its ancestors.

ℰnglish Toy Spaniel

Although classified as a "toy" dog, the English Toy Spaniel is more than a pretty face. It has been a successful bird hunter and was once known as "The Comforter" because of its gentle and affectionate disposition. It is said that an English Toy Spaniel accompanied Mary, Queen of Scots, to the scaffold. (Dog lovers will be pleased to know that the dog did not lose its head—only Mary.) The British coat of arms carries on its shield heraldic devices referring to the breed's long and proud ancestry, starting in China, moving to Japan and then Spain, before arriving in England. All this surrounds its favorite prey, the woodcock.

Field Spaniel

Another descendant of Spanish hunting dogs, the Field Spaniel has had a rockier road than its cousins, the Cocker and Springer Spaniels. The Field Spaniel was subjected to a period of experimental breeding that exaggerated its physical features so extremely that it brought derision from the public, and the breed nearly lapsed into extinction. The distorted features have since been bred back out and this, along with its hunting ability, has helped it regain its proper place among hunting dogs. It is too nice and intelligent a dog to have been left in that condition. The Field Spaniel crests a shield bearing heraldic devices representing its shooting master and favorite birds: pheasant, quail, partridge and woodcock.

58

Finnish Spitz

The Finnish Spitz is the National Dog of Finland. Fondly known as the "Finkie," it is widely loved in many other countries where it is primarily a faithful house dog. In Finland, however, it is also a prized asset of the hunter. Known as "The Barking Bird Dog," its vigorous bark assists in flushing grouse and *capercaillie,* a bird similar to the American wild turkey. The coat of arms of the Finnish Spitz contains the heraldic lion of Finland surrounded by the game it helps to hunt.

Flat-Coated Retriever

The Flat-Coated Retriever is not an ancient breed. It was developed in the late 1800s, crossbred from Newfoundland and older British stock. As an expert hunter and retriever, it was in widespread use on British estates and became known as "The Gamekeeper's Dog." Its shield bears heraldic devices reflecting its ancestors' honorable occupation as retrievers in Newfoundland fisheries, and the breed's current work as a bird retriever for hunters.

Ｆrench Bulldog

Whether this dog came to France from England or from Spain is a subject of great debate. To avoid controversy, let it merely be said that the little, flat-headed, bat-eared French Bulldog is much loved everywhere, including America, and nobody objects to its nickname, "Frenchie." Its coat of arms is the shield of France emblazoned with a French castle representing its high status. The dog serves as the crest and is supported by a pair of heraldic French Bulldogs. That's a lot of dogs, no bull!

LOYAL AND COURAGEOUS

German Shepherd Dog

Immediately recognizable and unmistakably a thoroughbred, the German Shepherd Dog exudes power and grace. This is a real dog—calm but alert, fearless, self-confident and rather aloof. Her appearance and demeanor are serious and convey the gravity and intelligence with which she approaches all tasks. Great willingness to learn and the desire to serve have made her a world class working dog. Initially, she gained fame as a herder and guardian of sheep. More recently she has excelled as a police and army dog as well as an outstanding seeing-eye dog. The German Shepherd Dog's coat of arms includes heraldic devices representing sheep and a farm gate. It is crested by an ancient Teutonic helmet surmounted by the dog.

THE UNIVERSAL GUN DOG

German Shorthaired Pointer

Here is a dog that quite rightfully sticks its nose in the air. Not only is this its natural hunting stance, but the German Shorthaired Pointer, also known as "The Universal Gun Dog," is probably the most versatile of all hunting dogs and has every right to be proud. The shield bears a sample of the many varieties of game it is adept at hunting.

RELIABLE AND LOYAL

German Wirehaired Pointer

Most breeds were designed for very specific purposes—flushing birds, stalking big game, running down rabbit, retrieving water fowl, baiting bears and bulls or even for fighting other dogs. The German Wirehaired Pointer, on the other hand, was bred recently to be a general hunting dog, well suited to both brambles and water. For such purposes, its coat was all important—a wiry, rough, water resistant mat to protect its skin from the harshest elements. Somewhat aloof, yet friendly, the dog makes a great addition to any family. It stands on top of an ancient Teutonic helmet cresting the shield of its coat of arms. The shield carries heraldic emblems of land and water hunters, along with pheasant and goose.

Giant Schnauzer

Long before the cowboys of the American West herded and drove cattle, the Giant Schnauzer was doing the same kind of work in Wurtemburg and Bavaria, without the benefit of a six-shooter. This breed drove cattle from the 15th century until the arrival of the railroad. Known as "the Münchener," this breed is dignified, calm, courageous and loyal. The Giant Schnauzer's coat of arms carries on its shield heraldic devices depicting the cattle and sheep it herded. The dog stands atop an ancient Teutonic helmet that crests the shield, which is supported by two heraldic bulls.

$\mathfrak{G}$olden Retriever

If it is true that the dog is man's best friend, then the Golden Retriever may well be man's very best friend. Her love of people, especially children, makes the Golden Retriever the extremely popular house pet she is. She was bred long ago to be a hardy, waterproof game retriever in the wilds of Scotland, but this may be overlooked by the many happy families graced by her presence. In her coat of arms, the Golden Retriever stands alertly above on a shield bearing the heraldic golden lions of Britain, supported by wetlands foliage. The motto emphasizes the qualities for which so many families love this breed.

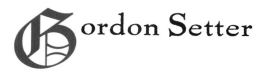

STRENGTH AND STAMINA

ⓖordon Setter

While most setters are extremely friendly and receptive to anyone, the Gordon Setter is a true Scot, reserved if not down-right suspicious of strangers. The Gordon Setter brings to the field not only great beauty, but also a smart bird sense, specializing in partridge, pheasant and woodcock. In its coat of arms, a Gordon Setter crests a characteristic Scottish shield on which a bird hunter shoots over a clump of thistle, which is a national symbol of Scotland. The shield is supported by two Highlanders along with a grouse and a pheasant.

APOLLO OF FREEDOM

Great Dane

One of the strongest and most statuesque of dogs, the Great Dane can strike awe in strangers just by his looks and enormous size. How he came to be called a Dane is lost in history, for he is an ancient German dog. He served his time as a war dog for German and Celtic tribes, and in the dark ages as a bull–baiter and a boar hound. He was named the National Dog of Germany in the late 19th century, the *"Deutsche Dogge,"* with the designation "Apollo of Freedom." As long as one does not have hostile intent or panic in his presence, he will respond with friendliness and kindness, although at times he does not seem to realize his strength. "Down, doggy" may feel inadequate when he is standing on your chest giving you mighty kisses.

He stands majestically atop his coat of arms, which has an ancient Teutonic helmet cresting it, wild boars and hunters as heraldic devices, and is supported by another pair of heraldic wild boars.

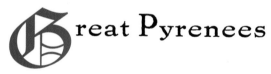

reat Pyrenees

Never judge a book by its cover, and the big, fluffy, teddy bear-ish Great Pyrenees is no exception. To look at him you would never think that he has been a smuggler of great renown. A native of the Pyrenees mountains since 2,000 B.C., he has had lots of time to learn the terrain. He was an absolute natural to carry contraband on his back across the border between Spain and France. On his coat of arms, this Great Mountain dog appears above a farm fence cresting the shield. The shield bears a heraldic sheep surrounded by the wolves from which the Great Pyrenees so successfully guarded his flocks. The shield is supported by a pair of bears which, except for color, the Great Pyrenees is expected to resemble as closely as possible.

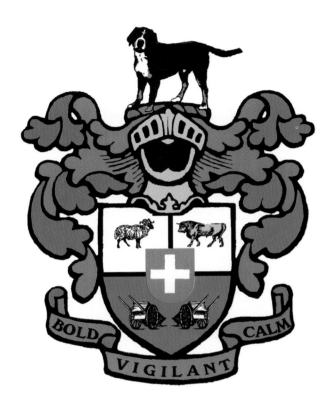

Greater Swiss Mountain Dog

The Greater Swiss Mountain Dog has been the number one working dog in Switzerland since its ancestors were brought by Roman soldiers centuries ago. She is a calm and steady friend to Alpine farmers, guarding and herding sheep and cattle, as well as serving as a draft dog, pulling produce carts to the markets. Her image crests an old knight's helmet surmounting the shield which is the national symbol of Switzerland. Emblazoned on the shield are heraldic devices indicating some of the breed's jobs.

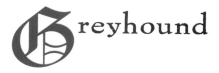

Greyhound

The Greyhound needs no introduction since he has been around for about as long as there has been recorded history. Through the ages, the Greyhound has been a special companion of the aristocracy. Though Americans have eschewed royalty, Greyhounds have been owned by many noteworthy democrats as well. General George A. Custer kept a pack of Greyhounds at all times, except (dog lovers will be happy to know) at Little Big Horn. The Greyhound's coat of arms bears shield devices reflecting his hunting prowess and some of his game, including his favorite—rabbit. It is supported by old heraldic sphinxes reflecting his ancient heritage in Egypt.

KEEP WITH THE PACK

Harrier

The Harrier is a miniature English Foxhound with much shorter legs. In fact, the Harrier's legs are so short that she cannot really keep up with horses while hunting. Instead, she became the perfect mate for those who liked to hunt, but would rather not race around on horseback jumping over stone walls. Combine this hunter and his hound with a type of game that is also not too swift afoot, the European hare, and you have the ideal combination (for the hunter at least!).

Jbizan Hound

Portraits of the ancestors of the Ibizan Hound have been found on objects in Pharaohs' tombs from as early as 3000 B.C.; one statue was even discovered in King Tut's tomb. This dog somehow got from Egypt to the Balearic Island of Ibiza where he has always been highly regarded. Hannibal liked Ibizan hounds so much that he let them ride on his elephants when he crossed the Alps into Italy. This dog is truly independent. Ask him to go hunting and off he goes, all by himself. He doesn't need a person to go with him to shoot the game. He will locate and chase his quarry to ground. If he loses sight, he leaps yards straight up to spot it over the bushes or just listens with ears like satellite dishes. In the end he pounces and breaks the neck, then gently carries it home to his master. His shield carries symbols reflecting his Egyptian heritage and the Ibizan coat of arms, along with heraldic devices depicting his favorite activity, hunting rabbits.

73

ℑrish Setter

There's something about this gorgeous redhead that turns the heart as well as the eye. The Irish Setter is one of the most beautiful dogs in the world. She is fully aware of it and can get away with the most outlandish behavior. That she is also an excellent bird dog is almost beside the point. With looks like that who needs to work? Her coat of arms is bedecked with shamrocks, an Irish harp, and birds she hunts or works with, in the case of the falcon.

Jrish Terrier

No auburn-haired temptress like the Irish Setter, the Irish Ter-rier is a feisty carrot-top who ruled the roost in farm yards where no rat was safe. Nor was any plump rabbit he could help bring home to the table safe from his grasp. When Irish troops went to war, he went with them and was as fearless as any in his duty as a messenger. In addition to all that, he is as good a pal as a child could ever have. His coat of arms has shamrocks aplenty, along with the Irish harp, a hunting horn, a rat and a rabbit.

CLOWNISH BUT ALERT

Irish Water Spaniel

Even if it does look like a poodle without a pom–pom, the Irish Water Spaniel is a distinct breed of ancient Irish lineage, although a Portuguese Water Dog may have crept into a kennel or two. As fearless as any of the other Irish breeds, this one is said to actually dive under the water to retrieve sinking ducks. Sounds like a shaggy dog story, and as such may account for this dog's reputation for a sense of humor. The coat of arms bears shamrocks as well as heraldic devices depicting the duck and goose hunting at which the breed excels.

Jrish Wolfhound

The Irish Wolfhound is large and robust, of cheerful disposition and, in shaggy tweed coat, certainly no dandy like the Russian Wolfhound. Since the dawn of time she has roamed the Emerald Isle hunting wild boar, stag and the now extinct gigantic Irish elk. She served her country in war, fighting alongside the very best. When she turned her attention to wolves there was no hope for them at all. Just try to find a wolf in Ireland today. The coat of arms is as Irish as they come and carries a wolf and a stag head. It is supported by a pair of Wolfhounds elegantly at rest.

ℑtalian Greyhound

Possibly the oldest of lap dogs, the Italian Greyhound has lived in the lap of luxury since Roman times, and with good reason. He is gentle, sweet, affectionate and the height of grace and elegance. He's a lover, not a fighter. He graces the Italian coat of arms, though he has been kept and adored by most of the royal houses of Europe and countless happy families as well.

Jack Russell Terrier

The Jack Russell Terrier is of recent origin and has been awarded a special shield reflecting the breed's importance to fox hunting. The shield is supported by a rendition of breed founder Jack Russell, the "Hunting Parson." This terrier is used to find foxes in their holes, from which she is removed by the tail so the fox can be let out for the chase. The dog does not seem to resent this undignified activity too much, although it is clear she would rather be left to end the hunt alone. The Jack Russell has been bred to have a lot of white in the coat so she is easily differentiated from the fox by both hunter and other, larger fox hounds. This has been successful, and the dog's head has never become a trophy as far as we know.

BELOVED PET

Japanese Chin

The Japanese Chin originally came to Japan as a gift from the Chinese emperor. In Japan they were kept exclusively by the nobility. So highly prized were these elegant and graceful dogs that they were presented to foreigners as thanks for valued services. Their coat of arms reflects the fact that they were cared for by the ladies of the Imperial Palace.

THE LAUGHING DUTCHMAN

$\mathcal{K}$eeshond

Just as the donkey and the elephant were adopted as mascots by American political parties, so the Keeshond was adopted by a Dutch political party, the Patriots, in the late 18th century. And like the donkey and elephant, the Keeshond was around long before the party. He served as a faithful companion aboard Dutch canal barges. Under Admiralty law, when a ship's owner was on shore, the Keeshond's presence carried the full weight of authority. A cheerful, happy dog, he is often called "the laughing dog," as his picture atop his coat of arms depicts. The shield bears the heraldic lion of Holland, and a typical old Dutch barge. It is supported by windmills, the symbol of the lowlands.

BLACK IRISHMAN

Kerry Blue Terrier

When the Spanish Armada attempted to invade England in Queen Elizabeth I's time, it was attacked by the English fleet and driven north in flight. Trying to escape, it came south past Ireland where it was struck by a raging storm. Few men or beasts survived, but those that got safely ashore settled down in the country. According to legend, the Spanish men and dogs mixed with the local blondes and redheads, producing dark haired offspring. These offspring with black hair have been called "black Irish" ever since. The Kerry Blue Terrier is one of them, which accounts for why its coat is so different from the Irish Terrier or Setter. His shield shows that he was a farm hand, a herder and a true Irishman.

Komondor

The cord-coated Komondor looks so much like the sheep she guards that she must be in danger of being sheared with them. This breed arrived with the Magyars and has been protecting herds in Hungary for over a thousand years. Because of her job, she has developed an independent, self-starting nature, always ready to defend the flock from all attacks. Perhaps this makes her a not-so-perfect house pet since she will view a mailman, a garbage collector and any other stranger with deep suspicion. After all, this breed has been driving off wolves and bears for ten centuries. The shield bears an Hungarian coat of arms surrounded by a flock of sheep and is supported by a pair of mounted Magyars.

𝕶uvasz

The word *kuvasz* means "mongrel" in Hungarian, but this is a misnomer—from his origins in Tibet to relatively recent times, the Kuvasz has been kept exclusively by the nobility as a guardian and hunting companion. He is a big dog today and used to be even bigger; his very presence was enough to discourage anyone with harmful intent. Later, farmers were able to keep the Kuvasz who served well protecting flocks of sheep. His shield carries the Hungarian coat of arms surrounded by boars he hunted and sheep he protected. It is supported by a pair of Magyars astride their mounts.

DEPENDABLE

Labrador Retriever

Although the Labrador Retriever was brought to perfection in England, it originated in Canada where the breed worked with the fishermen both on shore and on the boats. A real water dog, her talents were subsequently used for hunting—duck hunting in particular. There may be no retriever more talented, and she has strings of prizes to prove it. Her coat of arms includes that of Canada, along with symbols of duck and goose hunting. The shield is supported by two old heraldic retrievers, with another heraldic head on the crest.

COURAGE TENACITY

Lakeland Terrier

This tough, hard working terrier from the lake district of England was hunting foxes long before this was a popular sport. Foxes would eat the farmers' sheep, so the Lakeland Terrier came like a marine to chase them down and put them in their place. Because of its years of experience, this terrier was often included as a member of the pack in official fox hunts to teach the young foxhounds how to go about it. On the coat of arms a Lakeland Terrier stands above a gate, cresting the shield with the Royal Rose of England surrounded by hunting and farming devices and the animals he hunted. The shield is supported by another pair of foxes.

Lhasa Apso

One might think this little bundle of hair, the Lhasa Apso, would not warrant a "Beware of the Dog" sign. He was, however, a highly treasured guard in the lamaseries of Tibet. Ever alert and vigilant, he would sound the alarm when strangers approached, awakening the gigantic Tibetan mastiffs who would polish off the intruder. His coat of arms speaks for itself.

ANCIENT DOGGE OF MALTA

ℳaltese

There are many well known lap dogs, but the Maltese has to be the world's only sleeve dog. They are so tiny, soft and cuddly that ladies would carry them around in the sleeves of their dresses or coats. And the little dogs didn't seem to mind in the least! This was no passing fad either, for this breed has been around for close to three thousand years. Despite the name, coats of arms don't have sleeves, so this dog sits in a castle tower cresting the shield, which is that of his Maltese homeland.

Manchester Terrier

The Manchester Terrier reached the height of popularity in the Victorian Era, and because of its sleekness, grace and intelligence it was known as "The Gentleman's Terrier." This is an elegant and suitable epithet for a rabbit hunter, if not for a rat killer—the breed's other primary function. These pursuits are reflected in the devices on the shield which surround the heraldic lions of England.

BRIGHT AND GRACEFUL

Manchester Toy Terrier

The Manchester Toy Terrier is a miniature of the Manchester Terrier. More than just a little brother, he has been given his own coat of arms.

Mastiff

The Mastiff is said to have originated in Asia, then journeyed to Britain, and established himself there before the Romans arrived in 55 B.C. When the Normans conquered England in the 11th century, they called these locals by the French name for mastiffs, *dogues*. Because there were so many, "dog" was adopted by the English and subsequently all breeds became known as dogs while the English word "mastiff" also remained. He is a huge brute who is devoted to his home and family to such an extent that he cannot successfully be transferred to another. He is also highly protective of them, and big enough to back it up. His coat of arms fittingly shows him lolling on the front lawn of his house.

ℳiniature Pinscher

The "Minpin" may be a "miniature" Pinscher, but his heart is not miniature at all. Although he has been shown lying on silk pillows and bedecked with jewels, he is definitely no sissy. Lively and intelligent, he is devoted to home and master. His shield carries his image, and is supported by Teutonic knights carrying banners with the Germanic Eagle to reflect his origins.

M iniature Schnauzer

This bearded little dog was originally a small farm dog who gladly accepted the chores of catching rats and watching over children. She was also known to mind the cows and sheep on occasion. Nowadays she is valued as a pet, and in this capacity devotes herself with great persistence to playing games with her family. The coat of arms reflects the breed's working farm dog activities and Germanic origin.

Mutt

Despite vagaries of ancestry, a Mutt typically is a very proud dog filled with the high energy level characteristic of cross breeds. He is shown snootily cresting his armorial bearings which contain, appropriately, the crown worn by illegitimate sons of kings of France, as well as the very honorable and ancient heraldic device, the "bar sinister," which signifies bastardry. The Latin motto speaks for itself.

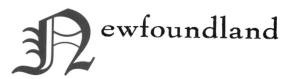

ꓠewfoundland

Volumes could and should be written about the New-foundland's service to mankind—from his relationship with the natives of Newfoundland and later the fisherman who arrived there to his heroics on land and sea, warning of dangers and rescuing drowning people. All that and gorgeous, too! Once in England, he was widely accepted and adored. Lord Byron's family honored their Newfie with a tombstone epitaph which described him as having ". . . beauty without vanity, strength without insolence, courage without ferocity, and all the virtues of man without his vices." He happily crests a Newfoundland coat of arms.

Norfolk Terrier

Norwich Terrier

This is the tale of two dogs who went to college. From their humble origins as farmhands who worked long hours chasing rats and foxes, the Norfolk and Norwich terriers were unexpectedly invited to university. They readily jumped at the opportunity, as might anyone destined to a life of killing rats. They quickly established their popularity among the student body, and so it was that they came up in the world. They are shown on a British coat of arms, along with the vermin they left behind. The Norfolk Terrier's ears flop over. The Norwich's stand erect.

Norwegian Elkhound

The Norwegian Elkhound is a mighty hunter as well as a fearless guardian against marauding wolves and bears. As the national dog of Norway, she served the Norsemen devotedly over the centuries and even accompanied Vikings on their voyages in the long boats. She surmounts the coat of arms with a complex shield bearing the Norwegian heraldic lion surrounded by some of the Elkhound's prey and an ancient Viking ship. All are supported by a pair of elk wearing medals of the lion of Norway.

Old English Sheepdog

The Old English Sheepdog, a.k.a. Bobtail, was a tax dodger, avoiding the British tax on dogs by having his tail cut off. This announced to the tax collector that he was a sheep drover, an essential job to get meat to cities, and was hence considered tax exempt. With his size, distinctive shaggy coat, and lumbering gait he stood little chance of avoiding the tax collector otherwise. Some may actually have driven sheep in addition to being much loved homebodies.

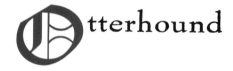

Otterhound

For over 800 years the Otterhound was employed by English royalty, including Queen Elizabeth. It is a well known fact that the English are fond of stream fishing and go to great lengths to protect their favorite fishing holes. The otter is a strong willed beastie that practically lives in the water and, unfortunately for him, also likes to fish and is extremely good at it. So enter the Otterhound! Big, waterproof, with the nose of a bloodhound and webbed feet, he once trailed a day's old scent over ground, then swam for hours following the smell an otter left on the water. Large packs were assembled to rid the streams of otters. The Otterhound did so well at this task that he ultimately worked himself out of his job, and the otter is now on England's endangered species list.

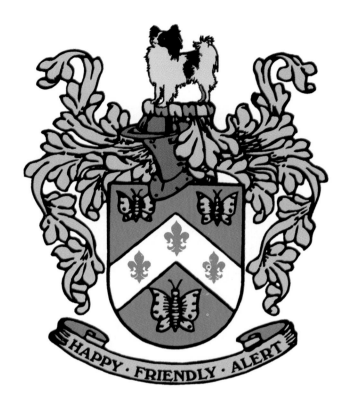

Papillon

The Papillon arrived in France on the backs of mules, brought by Bolognese traders who sold them for outrageous prices to the court of Louis XIV. Both Marie Antoinette and Madame de Pompadour were proud owners of these little charmers. This elegant toy dog with ears like butterfly (*papillon*) wings may also have had a purpose other than beauty—they are superb rat killers. Perfume was invented in this era to disguise poor hygiene and a lack of adequate bathing facilities. Is it possible that lack of sanitation also bred rats for which this pretty lap dog was the perfect response? The dog's very old coat of arms carries on it butterflies and the French *fleur-de-lis*.

Pekingese

While dog owners may occasionally complain that they are slaves to their pets, the Pekingese of the Chinese Imperial Palace had literally thousands of slaves with the responsibility of caring for them. Even before that they were pampered "guard dogs" of Chinese temples. The Pekingese has never done a lick of real work in its existence, and as it doesn't have the looks of Helen of Troy, the devotion shown him is no doubt the result of his great personality. As his coat of arms reveals, he is a pillow dog and considers acting like a lap dog beneath his dignity.

Petit Basset Griffon Vendeen

These small (*Petit*), short legged (*Basset*), rough coated (*Griffon*), French Provincial (*Vendeen*) dogs are otherwise known as "Griffs," "Roughies," or "Petits." In spite of this lengthy name, the PBGV ain't nothin' but a hound dog. His image crests a French shield of *fleur-de-lis* with heraldic rabbits. It is supported by ancient heraldic devices portraying mythical griffins, a pun characteristic of heraldry.

Pharaoh Hound

The Pharaoh Hound is as old as the hills, going back in recorded history at least 5,000 years to the days of ancient Egypt, and over that time has not changed a whit. The breed's pristine preservation resulted from its isolation from the rest of the world on the island of Malta starting about 3,000 years ago where these dogs were prized as the greatest of rabbit hunters. When she was finally given her due and made the National Dog of Malta in 1979, she had the grace to blush as she typically does when excited. She crests the coat of arms of Malta, which bears heraldic devices signifying Egyptian heritage and her favorite sport.

COURAGE AND DIGNITY

ℜ ointer

The Pointer is English through and through despite rumors that a wandering Portuguese Pointer crept into the kennel one night. Pure calumny! The Pointer is the role model for his style of hunting—he tirelessly and enthusiastically finds and points out hidden game birds on the ground in wide open spaces, then waits for his master to arrive, not moving an inch. Just don't ask him to go in a pond to retrieve—he really hates water. He crests his coat of arms; the shield bears types of birds he hunts surrounding a heraldic device depicting a hunting companion.

ℌomeranian

This dog is called the Pomeranian and his coat of arms is that of Pomerania, but it was in England, where the breed was first introduced by Queen Victoria, that the breed was popularized. Although he thrived there, he was bred to a smaller and smaller size so that he became dwarfed in comparison to his Spitz cousins.

Poodle

ℜoodle

This is not meant to be an odious comparison, but the Poodle has one characteristic in common with the pig: both hunt truffles. All similarity ends there, however, since the Poodle is much more than a root grubber. In fact, one would never guess by looking at the Poodle's splendid appearance that she could ever stoop to such behavior. The national dog of France, the Poodle is known there as the *Caniche*, derived from the not-so-elegant name Duck Dog (*Chien Canard*). Despite its beauty parlor appearance, the poodle is a talented hunting dog, especially good at retrieving birds from the water. Here she surmounts the shield of France, which is supported by a pair of old heraldic Poodles.

106

Portuguese Water Dog

The Portuguese Water Dog was actually bred and trained to *herd fish*! It is a waterproof, web-footed, tireless dog that worked aboard Portuguese fishing boats as far back as anyone can remember. The breed probably originated in Asia where a few were captured by invading Berbers and taken back to North Africa. The Berbers' descendants, the Moors, took their water dogs with them when they occupied Portugal in the 8th century. The dogs have managed to stay there longer than the Moors, so they rightfully take their place on the Portuguese coat of arms.

MULTUM IN PARVO

ℬug

The little Pug has had lots of fans for well over 2,000 years. Of Asian origin, this perky dog luxuriated in the Imperial Palace in Peking, branched out to Japan and then to Europe, all the time managing to get the best accommodations in the best palaces. A Pug named "Fortune" was the pet of Napoleon's wife Josephine. William Prince of Orange crowned the Pug the official dog of the House of Orange after a favorite Pug saved his life. The Pug's coat of arms reflects this history with a Chinese dragon, the Japanese chrysanthemum, the English lions and the French *fleur-de-lis* surrounding the royal lion of Holland. The motto, *Multum in Parvo*, most appropriately indicates that the Pug is a lot of dog in a small space.

ℙuli

The uninformed might think that the Puli makes a better mop than dog, but in fact it is a valuable sheep herding dog brought by the Magyars to Hungary about 1,500 years ago. Though it's not a big dog, it is nevertheless expert at its job and is said to ride on the back of sheep to direct their movements. Its solid dark gray or black color makes the dog easily visible among sheep. In the coat of arms the Puli appears cresting a shield that contains heraldic devices reflecting the breed's farming and herding background. The shield is supported by a pair of mounted Magyars and contains the Hungarian coat of arms.

THE AFRICAN LION DOG

Rhodesian Ridgeback

This dog was originally bred in South Africa, a cross between the settlers' European dogs and native African dogs. From his African roots, the Rhodesian Ridgeback gained the line of backward-growing hair over its backbone, and thus his name, Ridgeback. He is an extremely strong and brave dog that has been used to hunt all kinds of game, but was particularly valued for the ability to hunt lions with a human partner shooting from horseback. This feat earned the breed the title "Rhodesian Lion Dog." On the coat of arms, he crests the shield emblazoned with heraldic devices depicting some of the game he has hunted and a man shooting from horseback. The supports are heraldic wild animals of Zimbabwe.

110

Rottweiler

The Rottweiler accompanied the Roman Legions as they marched across the Alps to conquer Europe and, like many Romans, settled in Germany. Since the Rottweiler had driven cattle brought by the armies, she was easily able to get work driving civilian herds to market. Nobody tried to molest or steal any of her cattle and if you look a big "Rottie" in the face you will understand why. The coat of arms, which she crests, is supported by a pair of Roman soldiers. The shield is emblazoned with a Germanic Eagle surrounded by cattle.

111

WORTHY TO BEAR THE CROSS

Saint Bernard

The origin of the Saint Bernard is of less importance than his legendary feats of daring rescue. Swiss monks at the Hospice du Grande St. Bernard in the Alps raised these dogs to be guides for lost travelers. The Saint Bernard is a big dog in every way. His achievements include saving the lives of thousands lost in the Alps, holding the Guinness records for the biggest dog in history (over 300 pounds), pulling the heaviest loads and delivering the largest litter (23). He is truly an angel of mercy, which his coat of arms demonstrates. He crests the shield standing atop the famous brandy keg, even though he probably never carried one. The shield is emblazoned with the Swiss national emblem.

ROYAL DOG OF EGYPT

$\mathcal{S}$aluki

The Saluki may be the oldest known breed, going back almost 10,000 years. She was cherished by the nomadic desert tribes who kept her, and unlike the camel, she was allowed to put her nose under the tent and even permitted to sleep inside. She was a favorite hunting companion of the Pharaohs and is still considered the Royal Dog of Egypt. Once known as the Persian Greyhound, the Saluki is a swift dog who hunts by the keenest sight—like her favorite hunting partner, the hawk. She crests the coat of arms along with a pharaoh. Emblazoned on the shield are devices showing the Bedouin hunter on horse-back, the pyramids, and the Saluki's favorite game, the gazelle.

Samoyed

The smiling face of the Samoyed is not a mask; it honestly reveals his personality. He is a cheerful, enthusiastic friend to man and reindeer. He has never been expected to hunt and is not aggressive, though capable of defending himself if attacked. In addition to his herding skills, he is a mighty engine for dog sleds. Around the turn of the century, many Arctic explorers used the Samoyed to carry them across the tundra. His coat of arms shows dog and sled cresting the shield on which reindeer, which he so valiantly protects, are emblazoned.

Schipperke

Without a question the Schipperke *looks* Belgian. Relatively small and elegantly dressed in his conservative black suit, he has been the most popular house dog in Belgium. His title, which translates as "Little Captain," reflects his valued presence on canal barges. According to maritime law, he was the boat's acting master when the human captain was ashore. No one could board the vessel without the Little Captain's permission. At all times, he was the boat's rat authority, and a very harsh authority indeed. He is proud to crest the coat of arms, which is supported by a pair of standard-bearing Belgian lions. The shield is emblazoned with a canal barge, several of his arch enemies and a royal Belgian emblem.

Scottish Deerhound

The Scottish Deerhound, once known as the Royal Dog of Scotland, was described by Sir Walter Scott as "the most perfect creature of heaven." At one point in history, no one below the rank of earl was permitted to own one. So rare and valued were these rough-haired greyhounds that they could be used to purchase freedom for a nobleman sentenced to death. Masterful hunters, they were particularly suited to the wild highlands of Scotland. In the Scottish Deerhound's coat of arms, Scottish hunters stand on the motto that bears the Scottish thistle, supporting a clan shield. The shield is emblazoned with the dog surrounded by its prey.

Scottish Terrier

According to some, the Scottie is the oldest Highland terrier breed in all of Britain. Anyone who thinks differently should beware. This wee, black, bearded laddie is as feisty as they come. When the situation calls for it he is also a loyal, devoted family man who does his share of the chores, especially one that others would just as soon avoid—rat killing. However, he does have the disconcerting habit of depositing dead rats where his master will be sure to see them, like on the breakfast table. His coat of arms reflects his vocation and Scottish ancestry.

$\mathcal{S}$ealyham Terrier

The Sealyham was made to order in the 19th century as one Welshman's idea of the perfect terrier: handsome, small enough to chase badger and fox underground yet brave enough to hunt alongside Otterhounds in pursuit of their vicious prey. He crests his coat of arms; the shield is emblazoned with his prey and supported by a pair of the heraldic red dragons of Wales.

Shetland Sheepdog

The Shetland Islands of Great Britain might easily have inspired the Lilliputians in *Gulliver's Travels*. The horses (Shetland ponies), sheep and cattle are miniature because so are the islands and farms. Anything bigger would fall off the edges. The Collie was too monstrous for these tiny herds, so in accordance with tradition and necessity, the Shetland Sheepdog came to be. The Shetland Sheepdog is a perfect miniature, possessing all the Collie's good herding and protective instincts. Importantly, this breed is friendly enough to get along in small spaces. She crests the coat of arms which bears the shield of the Shetland Islands with three sheep emblazoned thereon.

119

LOVE TO LIVE LIVE TO LOVE

Shiba Inu

The Shiba Inu's Japanese name means (perhaps not too creatively) "small dog." This breed has been around Japan for over 3,000 years and has proved a swift and excellent hunter whom "you can never outrun." He is also a warm and friendly dog who is capable of "charming a stone."

SACRED PALACE PET

Shih Tzu

This arrogant, tiny, ancient Chinese Imperial pet has always had a pampered existence. Shih Tzu is Chinese for "lion dog," and this breed is descended from Tibetan temple dogs who frightened away evil spirits. It takes stealthy, smooth movement and lots of energy to chase ghosts and those characteristics have remained in the Shih Tzu through the ages. His beauty is also a major asset in preserving his pampered state, in which he is most contentedly shown on his coat of arms.

FRIENDLY & GENTLE

Siberian Husky

Siberian Husky is the fairly recent name for the Chukchi, a dog bred by the nomadic Siberian tribe of that name. The dog's purpose was to pull lightweight sleds over huge distances and help herd reindeer in its spare time. The coat of arms is supported by a pair of Chukchi tribesmen harnessing a husky. The shield is emblazoned with Chukchi dog sleds and reindeer.

Silky Terrier

Although classified as a "toy dog," the Australian Silky Terrier's enemies certainly don't consider her one. She most effectively eliminates rats and even snakes from the homestead where otherwise she is a friendly, affectionate pet. In contrast to Yorkies, distant cousins who modestly wear their skirts to the floor, the silky terrier wears hers shorter but still modestly, exposing her feet and ankles. The coat of arms is Australian through and through. The shield is emblazoned with devices representing her arch enemies.

WHA DAUR MEDDLE WI' ME ?

$\mathcal{S}$kye Terrier

Either the most loyal or the stupidest of dogs, a Skye Terrier is known to have stood continuous watch over his master's grave for ten years until his own death. On the other hand, he may have been the canniest, since he had no other family to care for him, and the good churchmen fed him regularly without making any demands! In the end, they even buried him next to his master with a fine gravestone at their expense. His coat of arms reveals his Scottish ancestry from the Isle of Skye and his favorite pastimes—hunting badger, otter and fox.

LIVELY AND PUGNACIOUS

ℭmooth Fox Terrier

Fox Terriers are old English dogs, once considered to come in two varieties, the wire-haired and the smooth-haired. Modern science has recently made us reconsider this, and Smooth and Wire Fox Terriers are now thought to be separate breeds with distinctly different ancestors. Even so, as their coat of arms indicates, they have both been illustrious fox hunters. Each breed crests his shield emblazoned with heraldic devices symbolizing their English heritage and fox hunting. All is supported by old heraldic horses, and the base reveals another expertise these terriers have—rat catching.

${\mathfrak S}$oft-Coated Wheaten Terrier

The Soft-Coated Wheaten Terrier is a self-confident, happy Irishman who has never been known either to pick a fight or run from one. Properly modest he is, with moderation in all things, excess in none. On his coat of arms, he crests a shield bedecked with Irish shamrocks that is emblazoned with the animals he has hunted for centuries.

Spinone Italiano

Dubbed "the thinker," the gentlemanly Spinone Italiano is an all around pointer of the old school. His mouth is so soft he can "carry an egg." He graces an Italian coat of arms that is emblazoned with some of his favorite prey.

Staffordshire Bull Terrier

Today, the Staffordshire Bull Terrier is known as a friendly, child-loving, fun-loving house pet though nevertheless a muscular, tough looking fellow who will defend hearth and home when called upon. English through and through, he was first bred from a cross of a Bulldog and an English terrier to be a fighting dog. That soon enough went out of fashion and he might have gone out with it had he not had such a good disposition. On his coat of arms he crests the shield emblazoned with old heraldic English lions and supported by a pair of bulls.

KINDERWACHTER

Standard Schnauzer

The oldest of the three schnauzer breeds, the Standard Schnauzer has been around long enough to have done it all. However, the only thing she has ever really hunted is rats— and she has been very successful. She is a versatile farm dog who can herd, pull carts, guard the livestock and family and last but not least, watch carefully over the children (her motto is the German word for baby-sitter). Her image crests an ancient Teutonic helmet on top of the shield which is emblazoned with heraldic devices reflecting her activities.

Sussex Spaniel

Although one of the oldest English spaniels, this breed is now very rare. Perhaps this is because the rest of the world has sped up, while the Sussex Spaniel has just gone its slow and steady way. The slow tempo was great when hunters liked to walk with a dog who would flush game for them, but this sedate fashion has gone out of style. He is a kindly dog and needs to keep his master in sight at all times. His shield is emblazoned with the English heraldic lions and samples of the game he flushes. It is supported by old heraldic spaniels.

Tibetan Spaniel

When is a dog not a dog? Or rather, when is a spaniel not a spaniel? Well the Tibetan Spaniel is a dog, but it's not a spaniel at all! So why the name? No matter. This little dog was cherished by Tibetan Buddhists as a "little lion" who brought good luck. The coat of arms pays homage to this heritage.

LUCK BRINGER

Tibetan Terrier

As the Tibetan Spaniel is not a spaniel, so the Tibetan Terrier is not a terrier. To make matters even more convoluted, some authorities say the Tibetan Terrier was never even a working breed, but only a valued companion and lucky charm to Tibetan monks. On the other hand, some experts state positively that the Tibetan Terrier is an ancient breed of herding dog whose instincts have been passed on to herding dogs throughout the world. In this case, the coat of arms will be allowed to speak for itself.

Vizsla

Although she's Hungarian, the Vizsla has much in common with an American from the deep South. She tries to trace her ancestors back in history the same way Southerners do, with just about as much accuracy. Perhaps she really is descended from the hunting dogs of the ancient Magyars, as her coat of arms indicates. On the other hand, perhaps the Vizsla is a relatively recent breed. No matter, for she is an alert, responsive, attractive and effective hunter; her accomplishments speak for themselves.

Weimaraner

The wonderful Weimaraner is sometimes known as "the gray ghost." Her gray color and amber eyes make a striking, sometimes uncanny impression even though she's basically an affectionate homebody. A native of Germany, the breed deserves the Teutonic coat of arms. The shield is emblazoned with the German Eagle, surrounded by heraldic devices indicating some of the animals she hunted. It is supported by a pair of stags which she tracked.

Cardigan

Pembroke

Welsh Corgi

Over 3,000 years ago the Celts wandered into Ireland, Scotland and Wales. It was only to Wales, however, that they brought a particular canine that they simply called "dog." In their Celtic language that was pronounced "corgi." These low slung critters dwelled in Cardiganshire and were especially good at driving cattle—biting at their heels to send them on their way. The Cardigan may or may not be related to the other Welsh Corgi, the Pembroke. There are many similarities, but some major differences as well.

And therein lies a tale. The cardigan has a nice long tail, while the Pembroke got the short shrift and is tailless. Since both performed the same farm chores, their coat of arms is identical, except for the particular dog cresting it.

Welsh Springer Spaniel

Here is another dog entitled to sport a Welsh coat of arms, though he's not really an old Celt like the Corgis. He came to be around the same time as the Cocker Spaniel, and for pretty much the same purpose—to be a good hunting dog who could flush game. His color (he is a redhead) is unique and sets him apart from others. His shield is emblazoned with heraldic devices depicting his hunting activities and is supported by the red dragons of Wales.

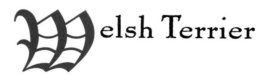

ALERT AND SPIRITED

Welsh Terrier

Every dog must have its day, and the Welsh Terrier is no exception. Though some people suggest he is nothing but a smaller Airedale, we say a pox on those who bear false witness! No dog has a better nature than a Welshie or is more effective in combat against otter, badgers or rats. He also has another charming trait that keeps him in shape when there are no otter or other prey to chase—he is particularly fond of swimming, with or without human company. He is also allowed to crest a Welsh coat of arms emblazoned with his specific heraldic symbols.

SPEEDY   HARDY   SMART

West Highland White Terrier

To look at him, you would never suspect that this pristine, pretty little tyke would even think about killing a rat. Yet the West Highland White Terrier is a terror of the rat community. Other than that he is a great companion who deserves to grace his Scottish coat of arms as the centerfold.

Whippet

Known as "the poor man's race horse," the Whippet was the thoroughbred who outshone all others back when chasing live rabbits for sport (and gambling) was popular. Partly Greyhound, partly English Terrier, he is an astonishing drag racer who can achieve speeds of almost 40 miles per hour in 12 seconds from a standing start. His coat of arms, with a pair of Whippets as supporters, is self explanatory.

![W]ire Fox Terrier

Fox Terriers are very, very old English dogs. Once it was thought that there were two varieties of Fox Terrier, the wire-haired and the smooth-haired. Modern science has made us reconsider this, and recently it has been decided that the Smooth and Wire Fox Terriers are actually separate breeds with distinctly different ancestors. Even so, they both have been illustrious fox hunters as their coat of arms indicate. Each breed crests his shield emblazoned with heraldic devices symbolizing their English heritage and the hunting of the fox. All is supported by old heraldic horses, and the base reveals another expertise these terriers have—rat catching.

Wirehaired Pointing Griffon

Although listed as a French breed, the Wirehaired Pointing Griffon has at least one Dutch uncle. Edward K. Korthals developed this breed in Holland. The Wirehaired Pointing Griffon was enthusiastically taken over by French huntsmen for its all around good hunting skills. The coat of arms, therefore, combines heraldic devices for France (the *fleur-de-lis*) and Holland (the windmill). It is supported by a pair of heraldic legendary griffins.

INTELLIGENT   SPIRITED

Yorkshire Terrier

The Yorkie is more of a purse dog than a lap dog. She is enthusiastic about riding around with her owner in any kind of container that allows her to stick her head up and look around at the passing scenery. One of her favorite methods of greeting is to race across the floor and leap directly into welcoming arms. The Yorkie *hates* being left behind!